Performing Projections

THEATRUM MUNDI

Contents

6   *Introduction*
      Cecily Chua

8   *Performance and Pedagogy*
      Jayden Ali and Andreas Lang

14   *What if all the world's a stage?*
      John Bingham-Hall

16   *Building Resistance: Performing the Reality of Life as Protest*
      Andrea Luka Zimmerman

26   *The Sensorial as Infrastructure: Making Pandebono*
      Andrea Cetrulo, John Bingham-Hall, Elahe Karimnia

34   *Performing Cultural Infrastructure 2018/2019*

38   *Queering the Monumental*
      Kleanthis Kyriakou

44   *Ode to SELCHP*
      Cameron Bray

48   *Allegory of the long spoons*
      Abby Bird

50   *Musings on the Market*
      Sara Lohse

52   *Spiritual Kaleidoscope*
      Lydia Hyde

54   *City, Building, Body*
      Annie Dermawan

56   *Sailortown: Sense of Place*
      Jake Johnson

58   *Performing Architectural Citizenship 2019/2020*

62   *If these streets could talk*
      Mollie Griffiths

66   *A Dance in 8s Interludes*
      Rebecca Faulkner

68   *Conduct to Conduct*
      Callum Brown

70   *Housework is work*
      Dhara Bhatt

74   *Multi-Generational Play*
      Awais Ali

76   *Tipping Points*
      Olivia Sutherill

78   *No properties, only belongings*
      Yibeijia Li

Performing Projections explores the two-year collaboration between Theatrum Mundi and Jayden Ali, Unit Leader of the Spatial Practices programme at Central Saint Martins. The resulting studio was an experimental testbed centred around one fundamental question: Can performance-making be a craft for architectural thinking?

Introduction

In the wake of Covid-19, we have seen cities across the world transformed into urban stages through protest, disrupting the cocoon-like stillness of lockdown. Within the current context, adopting a pedagogical approach to explore how performance based practices can amplify marginalised voices, reimagine roles, and invert power dynamics feels ever more urgent and instrumental. The arts are too often considered as an afterthought brought in to activate, decorate, or represent the city. What if they could be used as a tool to shape, reconstruct, or reimagine it? Can recording, scripting, moving, improvising, and storytelling shape the ways we think together the kinds of conversations we can have and the materials we can design with? These are the questions driving the work of Theatrum Mundi, the organisation, and ones we were lucky to be able to investigate with two cohorts of young spatial practitioners at Central Saint Martins in collaboration with Unit Leader Jayden Ali. We asked the cohort to reach out to and learn from the art forms that craft imagined realities on the stage to both reveal and intervene in the material infrastructures for culture.

We encouraged the studio's participants to shrug off the labels of 'architect' or 'designer', encouraging them to explore the city through the unfamiliar lens of the director, composer, choreographer, and performer. Discarding more traditional approaches to site analysis, methodologies were developed using the techniques of scoring, staging, rehearsing, and improvising to agitate, confront, probe, and cajole, raising provocative questions about who has the right to access, occupy, use, and remake our urban environments.

Combining the voices of students, educators, and practitioners working across the fields of architecture, urbanism, and the arts, this publication seeks to understand how the acts of researching, teaching, and performing, allow us to reflect critically on our own creative practices and positionality. Core to the ethos of the Spatial Practices programme at Central Saint Martins is the ambition to build an educational platform that reaches beyond buildings, beyond disciplines, and beyond borders. To do so, important questions must be raised by educators about who should be teaching architecture, and how we can move towards a truly interdisciplinary rather than silo-based profession.

Jayden Ali and Andreas Lang, who lead the Spatial Practices programme at Central Saint Martins open this discussion. Their free-flowing conversation explores the symbiotic relationship between practice and pedagogy, and the continuous loop they form of experimentation, situated learning, and teaching.

Theatrum Mundi's Director John Bingham-Hall's *What if all the world's a stage?* explores the stage as an extended metaphor for the environments we build in order to make and share in the constructed realities we call human culture.

Artist and Filmmaker Andrea Luka Zimmerman's *Building Resistance: Performing the Reality of Life as Protest* shows us a potent example of how the residents of a social housing estate who have been profoundly overlooked can resist media representations by voicing, performing, and re-enacting their stories and experiences on film.

Theatrum Mundi's Andrea Cetrulo, John Bingham-Hall, and Elahe Karimnia's *The Sensorial as Infrastructure*, borrows the recipe for pandebono – a traditional Colombian pastry – from café owners at the Elephant and Castle railway arches and uses it as a point of departure to reveal the underlying infrastructures of emotional and material support surrounding its production and circulation.

The following edition is organised into two sections showcasing a selection of the projects generated over two years by the students of our MArch studio at Central Saint Martins.

Performing Cultural Infrastructure experiments with methodologies and techniques derived from performative practices to explore expanding the capacity of the entire neighbourhood for cultural visibility and expression. What is the infrastructure for culture, and can it be designed into our urban environments? The studio sought to move beyond recreating the physical buildings or archetypes where culture is consumed, using crafts from the stage to uncover the hidden infrastructures, networks, and economies that support cultural production in the contemporary city.

Performing Architectural Citizenship explores the notion of 'citizenship' and how it manifests itself in our contemporary world of cultural collision. What does it mean to be displaced? We ask this in both the physical sense – to migrate, to cross borders, to seek refuge – and the metaphysical – to have your voice marginalised, to be disempowered, to feel your identity has been unrepresented or misrepresented. Using the city as a stage, the studio sought to uncover how everyday practices, rituals, and customs have been performed and enacted either in place of 'official' notions of citizenship or as tools to challenge, reimagine, and redefine it.

We have deliberately chosen to foreground the cohort's early-stage experimental work as a snapshot of the vast array of creative methods explored in the studio. From this disparate collage of stories, sounds, poetry, and scripts emerges a persistent question: if stagecraft can be a lens through which to see how public life plays out in cities, how does the design of the stage itself shape the crafts that inhabit it?

Cecily Chua, London, 2021

Performance and Pedagogy

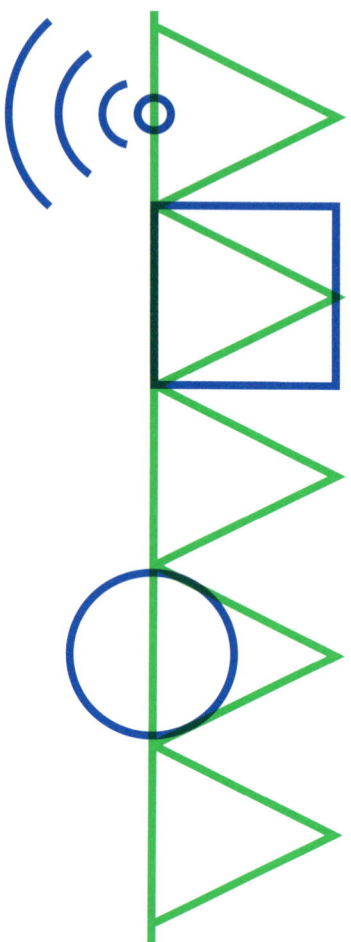

A conversation between Jayden Ali and Andreas Lang, who lead the Spatial Practices program at Central Saint Martins. Framed through their own experiences as educators and practicing architects, they reflect critically on embracing uncertainty, subverting the role of student and master, and performative practice as a pedagogical approach that is open to being tested, adjusted, lifted, and moulded.

Andreas Lang   I feel both of our practices and interests meet in performance from very different angles. Maybe we can start by giving each other a little recap about where that interest in performance comes from. I guess the reason I started teaching at CSM was that it felt like home. It felt related to my own practice, public works. Within public works, we often say that we work 'in the public and with the public',[1] suggesting a model of practice which occupies space in a very direct way by being present within it. Within teaching it promotes a pedagogy which is outward facing, encouraging students to go out into the city and immerse themselves within it, doing work within the live context rather than away in the studio. When I met you, the way you worked with the students seemed to echo your history as a playworker. There was a directness in your interactions with students which resonated with our embedded approach.

Jayden Ali   I remember, someone told me when I was working with young kids with behaviour difficulties that you should always do the opposite of what you think they want. If they're starting to make you angry, you should be really happy, and if they're making you happy, then you can afford to be angry because if you don't, there's a moment where they're dominating the situation. This is fine in some settings, but as a playworker your job is to construct scenarios that offer them something that breaks with their everyday, to offer them moments where they learn something new about themselves. That type of learning is often uncomfortable at first, but it's about becoming comfortable over time. I've also become comfortable with such discomfort because much of the world in which I've always occupied has never been in my control or my sphere of influence. As you know, I grew up in East London, where our culture is grime music and youth centres. I think exposure to that culture manifests as a kind of performance methodology, which allows one to reclaim or dominate space or at least be present within it.

AL   My own interest in performance comes from the idea that if you can enact an alternative, even temporarily then you are already setting up a space that holds different values to the dominant one. Even though it might only exist temporarily, it creates what Hakim Bey describes as a 'temporary autonomous zone',[2] where you can perform other realities, power structures, or dynamics in order to create a precedent or reference point. The resulting performative aesthetic in the case of public works is quite ad-hoc and low tech. Yours is different and is rooted in a different culture. It is not high tech, but technology certainly plays a role. You mix references including music, art, and history, imagining and referencing a black material culture. I think my own aesthetic has its roots in Germany, as I often feel in the UK things try to look familiar, try to fit in with a recognisable historic context, and my own work was always jarring with that. In this sense, we are both reacting against this; our practice have the same power of being disruptive. Perhaps I misinterpreted it?

JA I think you've captured that right. I remember working on the cherry trees (a primary school for boys with severe and complex emotional and behavioural needs in East London), where we did a big study about how children dominate sound. As part of our workshop, we constructed an after-school play provision where we gave the children a set of bells each. The bells were quite a simple thing, on a kind of pentatonic scale, which meant that however hard they rang the bells they would never be discordant – they would always be harmonious. All of a sudden, someone's gifted them a really loud toy, and they can make as much noise as they want, but it's not quite the discordance they are used to. I think that was the kind of moment that reveals my attraction to the methodology of performance because it distorted everyday power dynamics. It comes back to what you said about the students when they go out and set up a situation – it's a way to probe and to subvert power by experience.

AL I love the motto of the Artist Placement Group: 'Context is half the work'. It resonates with me, as I feel at least half of the students' work and learning is about practice. To me the art world, in comparison to architecture, always had a much stronger reflection on what one's individual practice is and what one might see as the identity of being an artist. It's the aesthetics as much as the resulting objects that embody the value system of the practice. I think in architecture and architectural education, we don't question the idea of practice enough because we often take it for granted. It's a service industry with a professional body, and there's a prescribed understanding of practice that is not being challenged as readily. Performance puts you as a person in the spotlight (you can't hide behind the computer), you have to understand who you are and understand what it is about your practice that feels relevant before you even get to the design of buildings. I think it can help you find your own aesthetic that speaks about what's valuable for yourself. By trying to find that, you often have to embrace a kind of naivety of the 'amateur expert' and the joy that comes with it.

JA When you said the word 'naive', it reminded me of 'ignorance'. Ignorance is bliss, right? And that's fine because you know we also exist in the world of dreams. Sometimes one has to be reminded of the fact that everything we do is a fiction, and within those fictions, there is the space to dream, and there is the joy of dreaming. Ignorant dreamers and ignorant schoolmasters. But I was also thinking that you could obliquely invert that title, and we could be kind of a 'Masters School of Ignorance'.

AL   I like that, and it will apply to students as well as tutors!

>JA   Maybe it's worth commenting on whether we think we're close to an established culture?

AL   For me, at the beginning and still now, what motivated me and created a strong energy around the course, was finding and establishing a culture which openly questions practice. What is it? How do we do it? Let's change things and explore things and test things! Sometimes it's just the joy of throwing things up in the air and reassembling them. At the same time, we want to be reactive to the different kinds of students that come through the door, and not roll out a formula but provide an educational journey that we refine every year. We are always trying to keep this ethos alive in how we create our learning environments, where pedagogy is something that is alive, continuously shaped, reflected upon, and practiced. I think this space is really something to value, as I see it as something quite rare. I think it's a form of performance in its own right. You perform learning.

>JA   To continue to riff on the idea of pedagogy, I feel like we're quite close to having established such a culture, but I'd be really interested to see where the course goes in the next couple of cycles.

AL   I completely agree. I think we talked about the threshold between decolonising and decarbonising a lot, and we want to position the course in the intersection of those fields. I think it's starting to happen through what you've been doing in the first year, which has set a really important tone. I'm looking forward to seeing that filter through the rest of the course. I trust in the openness and in the way we explored this territory on the course. After five years of running the course, we have enough confidence in its culture to embrace this direction. I think the next task is finding a way to direct our collective energy into these fields of knowledge which for me are: antiracism, decolonising, and social justice, which are of course very much linked to the climate crisis and biodiversity loss.

>JA   But then they're also just inextricably bound up in conversations around power. And maybe that's our thesis to play with and license to perform.

AL   Where do you think that energy has an impact at the moment? For example, of course, in the student's development. I also see the impact on practice, where graduating students start to bring in different sets of values into the workplaces they inhabit, where they decide to place or reposition their own practice. I also see it in the wider educational landscape, where it's starting to get more and more recognized as a unique contribution. So maybe it's worth thinking about in more detail where we want to have the impact in the next five years, because when you speak about power, I think we probably need to address power structures more clearly and what are the specific power structures we want to challenge?

> JA   It's a funny thing because if you use the parallel of constructing the situation, to use your methodology, one would be quite happy not knowing how it manifests. In some way, I'm quite happy because I think we've managed a sort of fidelity with the course because it is quite focused. I know the course as a whole is a strong project, but how it actually has influence or impact – I'm not too sure. If you'd asked me a couple of years ago, I would have said, I think it's had a positive impact in areas of policy sectors, etc., but I'm not sure I would commit to that now. I think it's at a moment where one actually doesn't know, and we should embrace that.

AL   Yeah, I do think it's not about indoctrinating students. For me, it's about empowerment and confidence and engendering a way of feeling comfortable with who you are, which creates a certain tone. If you indoctrinate students, you merely reproduce the mantra of the Unit Master (master architect) as the all-knowing, and I think that's the kind of attitude we actively challenge. Our students are really quite good at being in situations, knowing how to carry themselves, and are robust within their positions. I think their confidence comes from being comfortable performing, being out there and being in dialogue.

> JA   Maybe that is a methodology we should become more confident about because a lot of our conversations are about how we work on the output of the course. If I were to coach someone in public speaking, I would want them to put the finishing touches to their speeches, not for them to be copying the way that I speak. Perhaps that's the tension that exists because there is always this desire to pull back from the moment in which the students express themselves. Sometimes that falls in bizarre ways, but sometimes that falls in amazing ways. I suppose our role is to just equip them with the tools and the confidence to say what they want to say, not to predetermine what we want them to say.

AL   I completely agree. I do think we give that space; we don't set students up in competition with each other. There's quite a lot of solidarity and support between the students, and also support for their differences. That's really one thing they learn, to see each other's work through the other person's eyes, rather than measuring it against, say, the brief of the Unit. There's a lot in this setup and in the pedagogy that counters this idea of the master's voice.

I think what's really interesting is that there is an ongoing conversation and sometimes uncertainty in what constitutes architectural output on the course. I believe we should have confidence and accept that there is a tension about where the architectural output should lie, and I believe, to a degree, it is for each student to question and define it. We are very confident about the processes and the practices we nurture. It is also important to acknowledge that we are situated within an art school, and the methods we use are not necessarily quantitative but more often qualitative and relational, which sometimes sits in contradiction to the profession. In this sense, it's a much more fuzzy terrain in which to work. I think accepting that and owning it is probably really important.

JA   I just think there's value in being present in space. Just like there's value in children being present in situations. Just like there's value in my younger self being present in the built environment and expressing myself. By being present, you can engender trust, and you can build relationships. That is definitely what I think is important in our practice. Definitely for my practice – just by being there, good shit happens. And I think the course is present right now, or it has a presence at least. It's a good feeling.

AL   I think we should be proud of that. I completely agree with you. That's why we keep going to work and doing more work than we were ever asked to do. Because we treasure that space.

JA   Yes, it's a good space to hold.

NOTES

1   public works (2021) [www.publicworksgroup.net]
2   Bey, H. (1991) *T.A.Z: The Temporary Autonomous Zone, Ontological Anarchy, Poetic Terrorism.*
3   Artist Placement Group (2016) "Context is Half the Work" [en.contextishalfthework.net/about-apg/artist-placement-group]

What if all the world's a stage?

What if all the world's a stage? And all the people merely players? So, roughly, go the opening lines of the speech made by the character Jaques in William Shakespeare's *As You Like It*. A world with 'entrances and exits', in which we play 'many parts' throughout our time. Shakespeare's words are possibly the best-known formulation of *theatrum mundi*, a metaphor that has resonated throughout European literature and philosophy. A metaphor in which the theatre stands for the world itself, one used to describe its inhabitants as puppets on strings, to portray the visible realm as a poor set of shadows of ideal 'platonic' forms, or to disparage the charade of human drama as a tawdry performance of a godly script.

Religious moralising and metaphysical speculation aside, how could theatrum mundi help us now to think about the world, and particularly the urban world – the environments we build in order to make and share in the constructed realities we call human culture? How could the stage – as both a metaphor and also as a set of art forms – help city-makers build environments that enrich our shared realities?

But this in turn raises a question: can performance shape the stage itself? How might these crafts work back on the infrastructures that support them? Digging more into the metaphor itself could give some clues. What happens on stage? Bodies enact movement and sound according to designs encoded in scripts and scores; instruments, objects, and scenographies help to augment these movements and sounds, or their meanings; sometimes technologies, lighting, and digital media transform the ways an audience sees or hears what is happening.

Together, these are the crafts of staging; choreography, composition, sound and lighting design, scenography, writing, performing. What does it mean to be 'staged'? It could suggest something is intentional, but also that it is artificial or inauthentic, something that says 'this is how it could be' rather than something that simply 'is'. But these descriptions also sound like the built environment – a configuration of objects and spaces that, through the power structures and social ideas they encode, shape the ways we move, appear to one another, communicate, the roles we can play.

Uneven geographies of transport infrastructure are like scores that choreograph movement and encounter, whilst the stereotyped images of modernist social housing versus baroque palaces and faux Tudor mansions form scenographies against which social positions are imagined. So, on the stage, ideas of what bodies, characters, social archetypes, and reality itself are, or could be, are communicated through an interplay of reality-making crafts. Ideas made public through their encounter with an audience, in place or watching and listening via technology, become part of the shared public sphere of ideas about what can be. This is the core of the theatrum mundi metaphor – the blurring between the stage as a space to interrogate society and society conversely as something staged.

But I think we can and must now push the metaphor further. What is the stage on which these ideas, and the public sphere they form, are played out? Whether taking the form of a television or film screen, a radio, or the boards of a theatre, a stage is an infrastructure for attention. Whoever is occupying it is conferred the ability to communicate publicly to whoever is watching. Those who are on stage can be the public. Staging, then, is also infrastructure-making – building the technological or spatial surrounds that frame or raise up a 'platform' on which to reach the public. But the platform itself is not enough.

The stage is an infrastructure that has other infrastructures behind it. Returning to our metaphor, we can firstly think about the theatre as an institution. Communication, administration, fundraising, outreach, maintenance, and care work: these are the forms of labour that are not visible on the stage but build and sustain its ability to gather audiences around it. The stage itself is the end result of these processes and the people, the human infrastructures, who 'stage' the stage. Then, we can think about the backstage: the rehearsal rooms and green rooms where narratives are imagined and tested, where costumes are fitted, where scenographies are designed and built before they become public. But also, the physical infrastructures of rigging and equipment, and the people whose craft is to operate it.

So theatrum mundi, as a way of thinking about cities, points to an expanded set of crafts with which to analyse and intervene in a shared public realm. But deepening the metaphor, theatrum mundi also offers a way of thinking infrastructurally about the public. It draws attention to the layers of infrastructure, labour, and hidden acts of care and creativity that sustain a vibrant shared public sphere, as well as the physical systems and spaces in which that labour takes place. The final question, then, is how the crafts of the stage can help to reveal and intervene in the infrastructures that underpin them. In the context of architecture: can choreography, script-writing, and music production, for example, go beyond things that happen after the fact of building and become tools for working back on the material, economic, and political conditions of urban life itself?

Rather than answer this question here, I will leave the projects documented in this edition to propose their own responses. But I will return to the theatre once more for a clue. It is performance-making that has, over time, changed the shape of the stage and its container. It is experimental artists – in music, dance, theatre, and performance art alike – who have wanted to break down barriers between performer and audience, turning the stage inside out or abolishing it completely. It is those artists who pushed performance into new spaces, post-industrial ones, for example, changing our view of what a stage can be and the cultural geography of cities, for better or for worse.

These artistic experiments can drive, and must be supported by, transformations in the infrastructures of the stage: new kinds of theatre architecture or indeed anti-architecture; new kinds of art institutions and de-institutionalisation; innovative collaboration between artists and technicians to find new ways to bring visions to life. Could new forms of architectural practice – that conceive of movement, sound, and narrative as part of their primary material – similarly transform the spaces in which city-making happens and the spaces it can imagine?

John Bingham-Hall, Paris 2021

Andrea Luka Zimmerman
Building Resistance: Performing the Reality of Life as Protest

Andrea Luka Zimmerman is a Jarman Award-winning filmmaker and artist whose engaged practice calls for a profound reimagining of the relationship between people, place, and ecology. Focusing on marginalised individuals, communities, and experience, their engaged practice employs imaginative hybridity and narrative re-framing, alongside reverie and a creative waywardness.

There is no word in any traditional European language which does not either denigrate or patronise the urban poor in its naming. That is power.
— John Berger

I grew up here in a relief settlement at the edge of Munich. We were the first ones in. We had sheep, which was strange on a council estate, but we didn't have much else. I did have a social worker though, and we had lots of tins in the house. Let me just say that I have an ambiguous relationship with the smell of dog food, although I have a big dog. Today (5.1.2021) another old tree was felled in the name of progress. The 'Happy Man Tree' on the Woodberry Down estate was 150 years old, but got 'in the way' of a new block of flats. Initially, the developers thought that no one would care about it, and then, despite a major campaign, cited as the excuse not to delay a couple of months (when they could redraw the plans) that residents had been 'waiting for 20 years' for decent housing. The vast majority of these new flats will be unaffordable… Umberto Eco observed that one can use the same words in the same order and they can mean entirely opposite things. What is it in language that through it one can think but also unthink?

I   I have lived on the Haggerston Estate in Hackney much of my adult life, and for most of that time in the same 'Neo-Georgian' flatted dwellings as the old buildings on Woodberry Down estate, and here too the narrative for 'regeneration' was the same, that people simply deserved better… How many times can you hear this and still not know what it means?

II   This was Jeff Munro, resident of Samuel House, Haggerston Estate, for thirty years: 'I've got a little dog here, and my little dog has got more sense than all the governments have ever had. They're nothing but a load of thieves. Oh, they are! They're thieves. They're the ones that get away with those big crimes and the money. They're the ones! And if we get a small offence, like we diddle a bit of money out of Social Security, they come down on us like a tonne of bricks, but they can take millions. They can take millions, and they do.'

So how these mid-century flats are treated, flats that were once deemed luxury for their time and yet have been subjected to perennial underinvestment for decades means that the people inside them are ground down over those decades, because no repairs are done to fix holes in roofs or leaky windows, with all the damp, mould, and rot that follows… We were told that our buildings and our entire estate were unfit for purpose. We were told that it was the buildings themselves (not the administrative structures). The buildings were and are beautiful, and the people living in them are and were no different to other people. Yet the perception of both was to their detriment – abject housing leading to an abject people; sink estates that needed to be saved by the very governing hierarchy that ground them down. But we know all this. And yet, it keeps on being told, about council estates large and small…

1

2

3

4

5

6

III   These comments were taken from interviews with passers-by (my flat on the top floor, in the middle, Jeff's flat on the ground floor): 'Nobody lives there, nobody, nah. If they do, it's only a few houses occupied. They must be clearing it.'; 'It looks completely derelict, and I wouldn't want to live in it.' 'Frightened. Yeah, it looks a bit intimidating. Frightened and lonely because of all the, all the derelict, empty properties.'; 'Well if it was redeveloped, it would be all right. Otherwise, probably not quite up to my standards, I must say.'

Literally overnight, before a vote on the future of the estate, Hackney Council put orange boards over the windows of flats that they had just emptied and which they made forever uninhabitable by pouring concrete into the pipes. Our objections went unnoticed. There was a symbolic violence to that gesture. Living in a flat facing the canal, we could, from our open windows, overhear the stream of comments from pedestrians on the towpath, and we experienced first-hand how the estate had been turned into a bizarre tourist attraction – almost an early version of the so-called 'ruin porn' genre, evidence of the contemporary fetish for modern dereliction, a local 'Detroitification' that could be 'enjoyed', without threat, between latte stops. Suddenly people photographed the estate, not for its beauty, but for its abject quality. Orange as it was, the estate had turned into a projection screen for fears and prejudices about housing estates and perhaps even more, about those living in them.

IV   There was an urgent need among the residents to resist these forces, to respond in some way to what seemed to be an inevitable narrative, #ProgressIsComing. As the new buildings rose on these demolished plots– buildings with decent safety doors for the first time ever– we were told that we needed even more security. When they presented it to us, it seemed they wanted to protect us from ourselves, or was all this for the benefit of the incoming tenants and new owners?

Our rebuilt estate was hailed as 'the future of mixed social housing', yet what was mixed before is now segregated. We, the social housing occupants, enter through 'poor' doors. The private flats are all in their separate blocks, gated and with CCTV. You cannot encounter a 'stranger' now.

V   We can't precisely 'see' how power works, and mostly we don't even notice it until we are subjected to its full force. Power is evasive, slippery. The opposite is what power calls powerlessness, a feeling that accompanies the sense of being invisible, insignificant, a voice that does not count. This narrative of inevitability masks the conditions by which we end up in this dilemma in the first place, be it through laws or policy, the perversely impacting power of corporation and the derogatory machinery imposing a marginalisation of everything that does not fit this fable of progress.

Those that do not fit into these new worlds – be they the less wealthy, the economically disadvantaged, the drifters, the animals, anyone who lives a life that is not part of the productivity of these types of ideas – they are the ones to be narrativised as marginal, and difference is reduced to a place in the historical queue, whether that means the working class, the global majority, or all those not yet arrived in the promised land where, according to the law of capital, we should all be actively headed. This is what interests me: this movement, which is very subtle, of perception. So, for instance, the privatised city, privatised space (including quasi-militarised private cars, private healthcare, private everything), has as its mirror image the 'other'. It produces clichés and stereotypes that are reinforcing the idea of the abject and public fear, and which marginalise even further by making people feel unwelcome, unable to participate, in fact undesired: strangers in their own time and place. But should we be that surprised? After all, with working-class properties, once the roof goes so the house, and we're left with a landscape of history made up of solely 'stately homes' and 'seats' of power… Which is why so much of our tradition has been intangible, has been poetry and music. You can't lock up or tear down a song.

VI   Misconceptions about one another are largely structural, then internalised as if they were personal, inevitable traits or failings. It has so much to do with relatability. And misconceptions, of course, are shared across these intersections. This story of building resistance, in architecture and in spite of it, feels ongoing, circular, exhausting, exhilarating, depending on the type of mood I wake into. As we are starting another lockdown, I cannot but think of all those who live in cramped accommodation, without accommodation, in prison actually or psychically or domestically, without safety for their lives. Had I been locked into a flat as a child with a violent parent, I may not have survived. I cannot ever forget that fact. In her essay 'Narrative Reckoning and the Calculus of Living and Dying' (2019), poet Dionne Brand challenges this calling for 'when things return to normal' as if that normal was not in contention… 'Was the violence against women normal? Was the anti-Black and anti-Indigenous racism normal? Was white supremacy normal? Was the homelessness growing on the streets normal? Were homophobia and transphobia normal? Were pervasive surveillance and policing of Black and Indigenous and people of colour normal? Yes, I suppose all of that was normal. But I, and many other people, hate that normal. Who would one have to be to sit in that normal restfully, to mourn it, or to desire its continuance?' There was no 'normal' before this, and thus there cannot be a return to it. There has to be another way, building resistance.

Thank you to all the people whose journey I shared on the Haggerston Estate – our lives here have shaped me. Thank you for the campaigning and many conversations, and especially Gareth Evans, David Roberts, Ruth-Marie Tunkara, Lasse Johansson, Elam Forrester, Smart Urhoife, and Gillian McIver for our living and thinking things through.

7

8

9

10

11

12

Image credits

0 Andrea Luka Zimmerman (opening page)
1 Andrea Luka Zimmerman
2 Fugitive Images
3 Annotated *Hackney Gazette* cover (Rent strike Haggerston Estate)
4 Courtesy Nick Strauss
5 Fugitive Images
6 Fugitive Images
7 Andrea Luka Zimmerman
8 Residentwatch
9 *Estate, a Reverie* cast. Courtesy Briony Campbell
10 Filming *Estate, a Reverie*. Fugitive Images
11 *Estate, a Reverie* cast. Fugitive Images
12 Fugitive Images, film still, *Estate, a Reverie*
13 Fugitive Images, film still, *Estate, a Reverie*

Fugitive Images are Andrea Luka Zimmerman and David Roberts.
www.fugitiveimages.org.uk

The Sensorial as Infrastructure: Making Pandebono

Andrea Cetrulo, John Bingham-Hall, Elahe Karimnia

During one of our visits to Oscar and Valeria at La Caleñita, the café they've been running for nine years in one of the adapted railway arches at Elephant and Castle in South London, we were greeted with a coffee accompanied by a soft, warm, cloudy, savoury sphere-like bread, known in their native Colombia as pandebono. It was meant to be accepted as an act of generosity and hospitality in the vein of Marcel Mauss's idea of the gift, a form of exchange underpinning the formation of alliances and solidarity beyond self-interest.[1] It is through these dynamics of altruistic reciprocal relationships that La Caleñita operates on a daily basis.

RECIPE AS KNOWLEDGE INFRASTRUCTURE

The etymology of the bread in question is somewhat of a mystery, yet the most commonly accepted version is that it derives from the Spanish words *pan* (bread) and *de* (of) and *bono* (from *buono*, Italian for good), attributed to an Italian baker who used to sell the pastry on the streets of Cali, chanting '*pan del buono!*'. Another version is that it was named after the Finca El Bono, an eighteenth-century rural stately home in the small town Valle del Cauca, in Cali, where the bread originated and was sold.

The mythology and folklore surrounding its origins encompass a sort of syncretism that is reflected in the ingredients themselves: blending yuca (or cassava) and corn, both autochthonous to South America; cheese and butter made with cow's milk, introduced to the Americas by European colonisers; and the artisanry of the Italian immigrants of Cali who allegedly initiated its production. Pandebono is often accompanied by *dulce de guayaba* (guava jam) and a cup of hot chocolate, both tropical fruits that, as Gabriel Garcia-Marquez wrote in *The Fragrance of Guava (1982)*,[2] evoke memories of his childhood and permeate the imagination through their very smell. Smell as memory. Texture as memory. Vivid, tangible yet somehow intangible in the imagination. A glutinous dough that agglutinates individuals from diverse Latin American countries in a faraway city and acts as an infrastructure for sustaining everyday life. The amulet of the nomad, embodying both displacement and persistence at the same time.

When Valeria was prompted to share her recipe, she smiled and said, 'Pandebono is something that I relate to that time of the day in the afternoon before late dinner. I always had it at my home after school.'

PANDEBONO INGREDIENTS:

- Almidón de yuca
- Harina de maíz
- Huevos
- Queso costeño
- Mantequilla
- Levadura

Valeria describes her process:

- Mix all the ingredients
- Grate the cheese finely
- Knead
- Form bollos in your hands
- Make a hole
- Preheat the oven to 190 degrees
- Leave it in for 15 minutes (or so) until... you know...
- Tacit knowledge reigns. When it's ready, you should 'feel' it. Don't overthink it.
- Bake until golden

The way the recipe is enunciated is in the manner of an oral culture. Or alternately, a manual or embodied culture, that of the craftswoman who performs the task with mastery, yet also with an over-familiarity with the object at hand that makes it hard for her to rationalize and put it into words: '[it is] a process essential to all skills, the conversion of information and practices into tacit knowledge',[3] and 'what you know may be so familiar to you that you might take for granted its touchstone references, assuming that others have identical touchstones'.[4]

IMPROVISED ADAPTATIONS

Although this recipe travels with its makers as a kind of cultural heritage – already stabilised in form – it becomes the basis for improvisation when relocated from Cali to London, necessarily so. In Oscar's words: 'you don't find all the necessary ingredients here… Everything here tastes very different!'. Like other restaurants forming the Latin American cultural hub nested in the railway arches of Maldonado Walk, Oscar and Valeria source many of their goods from the neighbouring shop La Chatica, which specializes in importing regional products. But they must also resort to stand-in ingredients from the British supermarket chain TESCO, like the ersatz queso costeño, mimicked by the more readily-available feta cheese, or indeed, 'Greek-style salad cheese' – a simulacrum of one immigrant food, masquerading as another.

The import of certain Latin American animal products has been banned due to health and safety regulations in the United Kingdom.[5] As a remedy, La Chatica (registered as La Casa de Jack Ltd.) sells its own line of products that resemble the 'real thing'. Other delicacies, such as dulce de guayaba, are imported directly from Colombia in big batches and then repackaged in small quantities for sale in shops across Europe. Ingredients that are not produced in London are distributed and exported from Spain, an important Latin American migration node in the past three decades. The Spain-United Kingdom connection has been reinforced since the 2008 crisis when migrants relocated from Southern European countries to London, perceived as a better place for economic prosperity.

In London, one of the most popular food brands amongst Latin immigrants is Sol Andino, a Peruvian-owned shop with an online and high street presence at Old Kent Road in South London, a spot where Latin migrants live and gather. Sol Andino is one of the biggest distributors, catering to several shops and restaurants in the city. These kinds of networks of specialist food supply and consumption produce and reproduce this area of South London, stretching from Kennington to the Old Kent Road via Elephant and Castle, as a zone of Latin American culture. Unlike the specialist coffee joints of the aspirational middle classes (which no one knows exactly how to define but everyone can instantly recognise), this particular entanglement of food, culture, and socio-economics is focused around ingredients available in particular locations rather than aesthetics which can be reproduced anywhere.

Queso costeño, a soft, salty cow's milk cheese originating from the Caribbean coast of Colombia and a key ingredient in pandebono, is also made in-house by Oscar and Valeria themselves, which allows them to cut costs compared to buying it ready-made. 'The queso that you find here doesn't even come close to the one from Colombia.' In their café, this improvisation is also evident in the construction of the space itself. A railway arch, emblem of a very Victorian, very British kind of progress, is reconfigured as a mini-ecosystem of Latin businesses, from money transfer to the making of clothes and the making of pandebono. A lead tenant renting directly from the landlord – once the public Network Rail but now the private 'Arch Company' – has created

A recipe for coping

- Take a blank railway arch
- Provide cheap rent
- Adapt the space for basic needs and desires with simple materials
- Allow basic sub-divisions to be made without requiring permissions
- Allow subtenants to add the finishing touches

sub-lettable units through simple plywood partitions, which have in turn been adapted by their own tenants for a multitude of uses. What makes this place 'Latin American', or in La Caleñita's case, Colombian? Language, smells, tastes, sounds from the TV. Things that cannot be made through architecture, but through use. However, it is not only the sensorial environment that constitutes a cultural space but the way of producing it.

A RECIPE FOR COPING

Informality and self-reliance have travelled in the bodies of people like Oscar and Valeria, another unwritten recipe allowing local spatial ingredients to be recooked into something distinct and culturally enriching. As a La Caleñita habitué puts it '[pandebono] brings memories of driving to the outskirts of Bogotá to have it on Sundays with my family when I was a child. It's like you need to know it. Visually it's not appealing; you need to feel it. I personally love the warmth and elasticity of it.' Another customer from Chile, new to the place, inquires about the different baked goods displayed on the counter at La Caleñita, unsure of which one to pick: 'I am Chilean, but there are so many commonalities between Latin Americans anyways, it feels like home.' These often unspoken, shared codes are held together by what Benedict Anderson coined 'imagined communities',[6] the idea of a Pan Latin American community based on affinity brought by the peculiar needs of relocation and infrastructures of coping.

In Oscar's words: 'This place acts as a social hub, not only a restaurant. When a new migrant [from Latin America] arrives with just a suitcase and nowhere to go, we provide them with food and shelter. This pays back, as they always return once their situation gets better.' Pandebono fulfils a social function and enhances the power of imaginations through the sensorial, acting as a pillar for coping with the vicissitudes of instability. When it's consumed, it elicits memories of place, bringing to mind that 'all really inhabited space bears the essence of the notion of home'.[7]

Coping is a creative act, an improvisational activity, an attitude towards the world of uncertainties, focussing on opportunities, and forging solidarity. Migrants coping with structured inequalities in everyday life highlight their creative and experimental performance as they go; no matter that Oscar and Valeria can't get the same ingredients for pandebono in London, they are confident in themselves and their community for finding alternative resources and mutual support.

Pandebono cannot be simply reduced to a recipe of ingredients, like those attempted at formulating context-free suggestions for the problems our cities deal with. The recipe, rather than a prescriptive form, becomes support for a kind of improvisation that allows the immigrant to reconfigure the unfamiliar materials of the host country into an embodiment of home. It is an organising framework that allows unrelated elements – Greek-style salad cheese, yucca, British eggs – to participate in the construction of something not constituted by any one of them individually but by their relationships.

COOKING AND INFRASTRUCTURING

What do we learn from pandebono, then, about culture and its infrastructure, the conditions that enable those without institutional or political power to make and remake the city? Like recipes, infrastructures can be used to enable or to constrain. If they fix a set of pre-defined elements so rigidly that the malfunctioning or unavailability of one of them invalidates the whole structure, they bring about situations of control and redundancy. We can think of 'recipes' for cultural regeneration in the Bilbao model, built around a 'flagship' museum, preconceived from building to programme. If the museum does not work, both itself and its surrounding 'cultural district' can become deserted wastelands, unable to be rethought and readapted from the bottom up by virtue of being designed for institutional-scale actors. Like the proverbial soufflé in which one failure renders the whole thing useless, such masterplanning is what Sennett calls 'closed' or 'complete form'[8]. Alternately, recipes can be 'open forms', organising frameworks choreographing a set of relationships between interchangeable elements, a way of passing on ideas and methods for making form with the materials to hand. This points to a different kind of cultural planning in which a broad set of infrastructures are understood, and individuals and small collectivities make their own forms of cultural space, which then become infrastructures for other things, like sensing and coping.

For Oscar and Valeria, and other members of their community, improvisation is essential when working with this lack of overarching plan or institutional structure – in a state of 'unincorporation'[9] – and without the imposition of a 'design' that predetermines the aesthetic end-point. This is evident in the social support structures that have emerged around the informally adapted infrastructure of the arches on Maldonado Walk.

Improvisation is helping to find last-minute accommodation for newcomers, or covering shifts with short notice, or assisting each other with moving house, or setting up an impromptu shelter in the kitchen for anyone who needs it. Improvisation is plastering the wall of a dim, austere cave-like structure under a railway station with the picture of a tropical beach, feeding not only the stomachs but also the imaginations of those who gather in here. But improvisation does not happen in a vacuum. As scores can provide a shared basis on top of which performers improvise with sound and movement,[10] infrastructural recipes made of knowledge, space, material, and planning policy are the solid ground that enables immigrant makers to improvise with and gain agency over urban form.

Despite the undeniable power that comes with the migrant's ability to reconstruct, remodel, and reshape new microcosms for herself and others around her, recent regeneration strategies for the area, which include the imminent sale of the railway arches to private investors, threaten the continuity of these accessible spaces for the production of goods and immaterial affective support structures. Where there is a strong reliance on the space of place, can a place like this be swept away in its materiality without dragging with it the lifeworld of those who inhabit it?

ACKNOWLEDGMENT

This is part of Theatrum Mundi's research project *Urban Backstages*, investigating the conditions of cultural production in Paris, Marseille, Glasgow, and London with support from the Ax:son Johnson Foundation. The research is conducted by John Bingham-Hall, Andrea Cetrulo, Cecily Chua, Elahe Karimnia, Fani Kostourou, and Justinien Tribillon.

NOTES

1. Mauss, M. (1954) *The Gift: The Form and Reason for Exchange in Archaic Societies.*
2. García Márquez, G. and Mendoza, P. (1983) *The Fragrance of Guava.*
3. Sennett, R. (2008) *The Craftsman.*
4. Ibid.
5. *Importing live animals, animal products and high risk food and feed not of animal origin from non-EU countries to Great Britain* (2015). [gov.uk/guidance/importing-live-animals-or-animal-products-from-non-eu-countries]
6. Anderson, B. (1983) *Imagined Communities.* Reprint, Verso, 2006.
7. Bachelard, G. (1958) *The Poetics of Space.*
8. Sennett, R. (2019) *Building and Dwelling.*
9. Bingham-Hall, J., Chua, C., Cetrulo, A., and Ali, J. (2019)*Urban Backstages: Unincorporated Artists Unite.*
10. Bingham-Hall, J. (2019) *What kind of thing is a score?* [theatrum-mundi.org/library/what-kind-of-thing-is-a-score]

The following section showcases a selection of the projects generated over two years by the students of our MArch studio at Central Saint Martins. Drawing from the crafts of the stage, these experiments in choreography, dramaturgy, storytelling, music, and poetry bridge the worlds of city making and the performing arts to conceive new forms of architectural practice. Collectively, the works foreground movement, sound, and narrative as the tools for reimagining our urban environments.

Performing Cultural Infrastructure

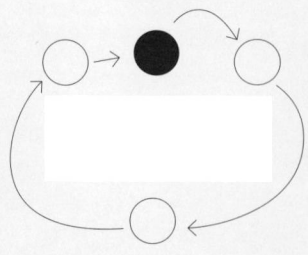
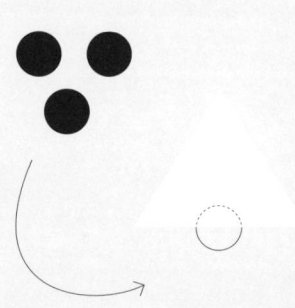
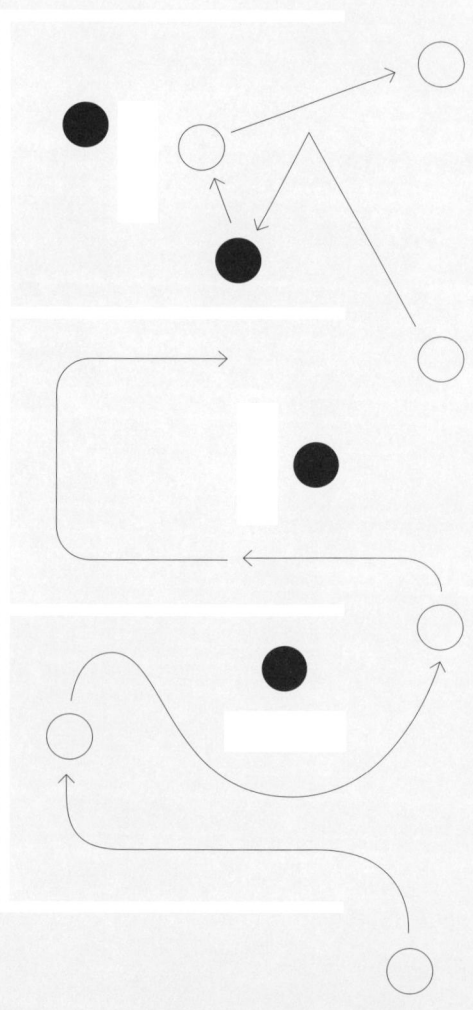

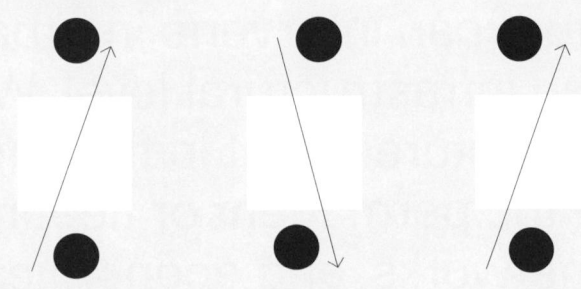

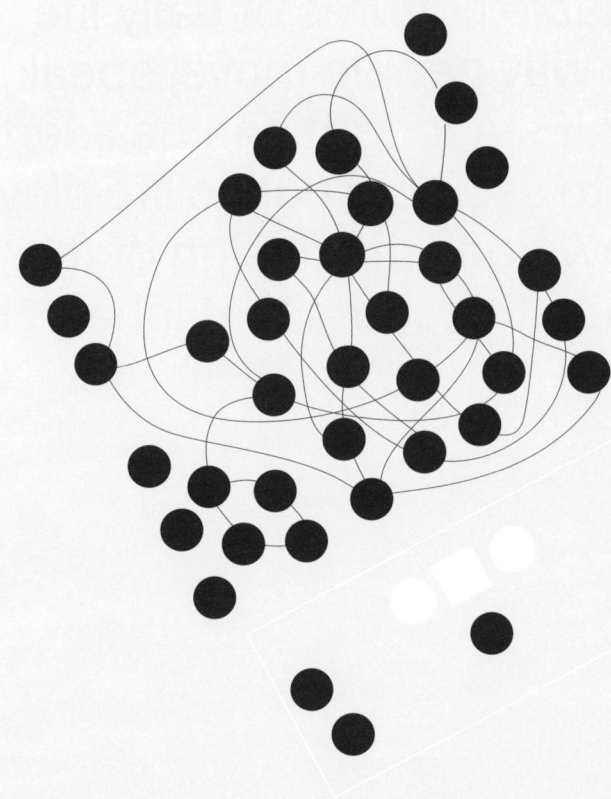

Performing Cultural Infrastructure investigates the ways in which architecture can intervene in urban culture at an infrastructural level. Where do infrastructures exist in the contemporary city – the permanent or fleeting processes, networks, and economies which come together to facilitate a particular behaviour, lifestyle, or expression? How do the underlying infrastructural conditions of the city constrain or enable cultures of daily life in a place – the way people move, speak, eat, and dress? If stagecraft can be a lens through which to see how public life plays out in cities, how does the design of the stage itself shape the crafts that inhabit it?

Kleanthis Kyriakou
Cameron Bray
Abby Bird
Sara Lohse
Lydia Hyde
Annie Dermawan
Jake Johnson

2018/2019

Kleanthis Kyriakou *Queering the Monumental*

The global Black Lives Matter movement and the ongoing protests to take down troublesome (contested) urban monuments are striving to redress narratives imposed on our cities. The killing of George Floyd in late May, an African American, during an arrest in Minneapolis, sparked a series of anti-racism protests in major cities around the world, transcending national barriers and defying lockdown measures imposed by Covid-19. In the UK, a country that serenades its imperial past in its national anthem, the legitimacy of monuments dedicated to colonial-era slave traders has come to the forefront of sociopolitical debate. The scenes that unfolded in Bristol during a Black Lives Matter demonstration on June 7th were in equal measure preposterous and exhilarating.

An effigy of slave trader Edward Colston located in the city centre was overthrown and dragged through the streets into its watery grave, in the nearby harbour. The act, which attracted worldwide media attention and was described as 'thuggery' by the Home Secretary Priti Patel,[1] prompted (the beginning of) the removal of many other sculptures depicting those that benefited from racial violence. In London, Mayor Sadiq Khan has promised that every monument with colonial slave trade associations will fall.

Racism has had material presence and manifestations in urban space for centuries, in our very own streets and squares, sometimes carved in stone, sometimes cast in bronze. As the wave of protests continue in London, graffiti, or more precisely political inscriptions, have appeared on sculptures around Whitehall, the central meeting ground for the demonstrations. The monument to the nation's most admired political figure, Sir Winston Churchill, was one of the victims. Following this incident, key statues around Whitehall have been boarded up, braced, and concealed. London's historical elite have become invisible, monuments to no one, hidden inside wooden crates. While peaceful demonstrations proceeded, police force was employed to actively protect those monuments against destruction, highlighting their importance to the state and the calibre of the ruling power.

As the city is turning into a blank canvas, its colonial era monuments removed or boarded up, forming allegorical plinths for new monuments to be erected, is it time for minorities to claim their own permanence in the city, to immortalise our own histories, beliefs, and ideals? This question truly resonates with my own practice as a queer architect and performer. In my work, I am dissecting queer fragility and looking at ways to preserve and memorialise London's queer heritage.

Lesbian, gay, bisexual, trans, and queer (LGBTQ+) histories are rooted in the buildings and landscapes all around us. Historic England hosts an extensive catalogue of LGBTQ+ sites in its online database, Pride of Place, ranging from the underground members clubs of the West End to the Public Courts where queers were trialled and persecuted over indecent acts. But much like the monuments in Whitehall, these stories are covered up and hidden.

Huge eighteenth-century mansions built as safe havens for their closeted patrons, the pubs, bars, and clubs that we lost deserve to be remembered for their contribution to London's collective queer psyche. Spaces like the Joiners Arms, a notorious LGBTQ+ pub in East London, permanently shut its doors in 2015, despite community efforts to re-establish it.

† What is a monument?
† Who benefits from public monuments?
† Who has a right and agency over them?
† Who and what do we choose to memorialise as a society?

In Southwark, XXL – London's premier gay nightclub that counted 100,000 members – presented its final night in September 2019. London, a city credited as the most progressive on Earth by the mayor's office, continues to witness the rapid loss of its LGBTQ+ establishments, in part due to gentrification and the rise of online dating apps. According to a 2018 study led by Ben Campkin and Laura Marshall of UCL's urban laboratory, London has lost 56% of its LGBTQ+ premises in the last decade alone, with councils such as Tower Hamlets losing an alarming 70% of those spaces.[2] I propose to seize this moment of change and radically rethink the potential for a decolonised public space – one where the queer minority can have a concrete presence.

During the Swinging Sixties, shortly after the relaxation of post-war austerity measures, the abundance of empty spaces in London's city centre provided a platform for LGBTQ+ venues to emerge. Yet ownership was temporary, as urban space has predominantly been driven by capital. Soho for instance, the city's infamous 'gaybourhood' has been reduced to an array of homogeneous luxury trainers shops, as seen on the district's Brewer street – once famed for its sex shops and cabaret nights. By using the typology of the monument to redress the impermanence that defines queer urban space, I aim to reveal alternative histories and grant the LGBTQ+ community a permanence in the built environment that other cultural or religious groups enjoy. Potential Monuments is influenced by The Church Ladies for Choice – a vocal group of crossdressers that built their own monuments to protest the lack of AIDS treatment and anti-abortion laws in the late 1980s in New York City.

My finished pieces are not solely static representations of an idea, immobile statues; they are openings for performances, led by my drag alter ego Divine III. In Potential Monuments, a plinth, an altar, a tower, and a dress become shrines to London's lost queer spaces. Unlike the sculptures depicting the male slave-traders, my monumental propositions do not represent the dominance of the oppressor but instead allow for diverse voices of the oppressed to be heard, loud and clear.

NOTES

1 Duncan, C. (2020) 'London protests: Priti Patel condemns "unacceptable thuggery" as statue demonstrators clash with police' *The Independent* [independent.co.uk/news/uk/politics/london-protests-priti-patel-churchill-statue-today-latest-a9564556.html]
2 Campkin, B. and Marshall, L. (2017) *LGBTQ+ Cultural Infrastructure in London: Night Venues*, 2006-present [ucl.ac.uk/urban-lab/research/research-projects/lgbtq-nightlife-spaces-london]

3

4

1   *A monument to Strawberry Hill* (2020)
    Plywood, plaster, glitter

This towering monument pays homage to the queer mythologies of Strawberry Hill House and its patron Horace Walpole. Walpole was a queer man, writer, architect, socialite, and the son of the UK's first prime minister. In 1749, he envisioned Strawberry Hill House in Twickenham – a suburban palace built in the Gothic style, at a time when Palladianism was still in fashion. Inside his secluded mansion, he created a world of his own, where he could explore his identity free from prying eyes. The Neo-Gothic of Strawberry Hill can be understood as a camp act of defiance against the status quo. This act of queer architectural rebellion is not any less relevant today, where we encounter the replacement of LGBTQ+ spaces with towering glass architecture. Strawberry Hill has been preserved as a cultural edifice of the past, yet stripped from its queer narrative. By queering some of Strawberry Hill's Gothic elements, the monument seeks to revive its memory as a safe space for gender ambiguity. Scaled-down casts of its facade are embellished with glitter and feathers, whereas the traditional four-pillar colonnade, found in the house's lush interior, gets a twisted makeover, representing bodies during sexual intercourse.

2   *A memorial for XXL*, (2020)
    Aluminum, chrome, MDF

Inspired by the typology of religious altars, *A memorial for XXL* is a manifestation of the gay nightclub located in Southwark, South London. XXL was a temple for London's bear and leather communities for almost two decades, before its closure in 2019. The terms 'bear' and 'leather' correspond to sub-cultures within the gay community that respond to physical characteristics or sexual preferences. Although controversial because of its strict door policy that rejected any visible signs of femininity, XXL held a special place in London's gay scene as the last remaining super club equipped with a labyrinthine dark room. The altar amplifies the spatial characteristics of XXL, private and hidden from passers-by.

The focal point of the monument lies in its medial circular opening. The circle itself 'glorifies' the gloryhole, a symbol of transgressive sexuality. Alongside its symbolic representation, it enables mourners to pay their respects by placing their offerings through it. A chrome weight bar invites mourners to participate in a fitness ritual, associated with XXL's former clientele.

3   *A political dress* (2020)
    Acrylic paint on silk

In this piece, the body itself becomes a monument. A living, breathing monument. Positioned at the top of a ladder, it demands attention and respect. A five-metre-long silk dress is draped around the body, all the way to the floor. Its purpose is to serve as a wearable protest banner inscribed with a message that is prevalent throughout my design work: 'Save London's Queer Spaces'. The message was graffitied on the dress as if protesters have added it during a demonstration. However, in this case, it is not considered an act of vandalism but a call for action!

4   *The Queer Plinth* (2019)
    Plaster, silicone, MDF

Envisaged as a monument to queer culture, it is designed to permanently occupy the Fourth Plinth in Trafalgar Square, a host to ephemeral contemporary monuments since 1999. Responding to the multitude of LGBTQ+ nightlife closures, the monument acknowledges the importance of LGBTQ+ spaces as enclaves for gender performativity and our right to claim space within the city. Trafalgar Square is the site of the annual Pride celebrations in London, and at times of unrest, a site of civic occupation. Thus, the potential of a long-lasting monument to 'Queer culture' in the civic heart of London is extremely powerful. The form of the plinth takes its cues from ancient Greek architecture, appropriated and reworked to represent the fragility and the unstable upbringing of our ancestors.

Its base bears the caption *Non Satis Recte*, translated from Latin as 'Not Quite Right', which was one of the first definitions of the word 'queer' when it first emerged in the fifteenth century. The Queer Plinth has been used as a prop for an imaginary funeral for the Joiners Arms, the legendary LGBTQ+ pub on Hackney Road, which was forced to shut its doors in 2015. A flower wreath completes the composition, referencing the use of monuments as places to commemorate significant historical events, while at the same time drawing parallels with East End funeral traditions.

Cameron Bray *Ode to SELCHP*

I was born in November 1994, on Surrey Canal Road, between South Bermondsey and Deptford. I grew up nestled between a knot of railway lines, an industrial estate, and the Millwall stadium.

I'm known for my energy. I've got what they call a fire in my belly, although my diet isn't great - I eat a lot of junk food. To be honest, I'm not all that healthy - I smoke quite a bit too.

But anyway, like I said, I'm very industrious. Every day, I burn about 1,200 tonnes of rubbish. Bin lorries from three London boroughs queue up outside my gate around lunchtime, and I turn their waste into electricity with this massive turbine, which can power about 48,000 homes.

I've also made a deal with Southwark Council, meaning that I reroute all the heat made by the burning rubbish, and this keeps 2600 homes warm in winter time. Judging by the internet forums, I'm not brilliant at that though - apparently the district heating is broken half the time.

I am actually a bit of a controversial figure... Some Greenpeace activists climbed up my chimney once and shut me down for three days. You know what though? I'm very transparent about my emissions, and they do meet all European standards... But I'm not perfect.

I've got some pretty good friends - there are loads of other recyclers nearby, and there's a big industrial estate next door with all kinds of cool stuff going on. The best neighbour is the Millwall stadium though - that lot know how to have a good time!

I'm quite tall - 100 metres in fact. I'm actually taller than all the buildings in Lewisham. You could call me a landmark. I've been told I guide people home at night, which is a nice compliment. It's weird though, because a lot of people seem to ignore me too. What they don't realise is that every time they turn on the kettle, or turn up the heating, I'm there behind the scenes, keeping everything going, like a conductor and their orchestra.

Anyway, Got to run, nice to meet you. My name is South East London Combined Heat and Power, but you can call me SELCHP (that's Sell-Chip).

Format	Performance using field recordings, spoken word, video and a kettle
Location	Surrey Canal Road, London

Ode to SELCHP layers the sounds of a power station with the boiling of a kettle. Personifying the power plant, the performance traces the invisible relationship between the places that make electricity and the things that use it – an industrial-domestic mashup. The sounds are layered to build a wall of noise, until the kettle clicks off the boil and everything goes silent as the performer makes a cup of tea.

Abby Bird *Allegory of the long spoons*

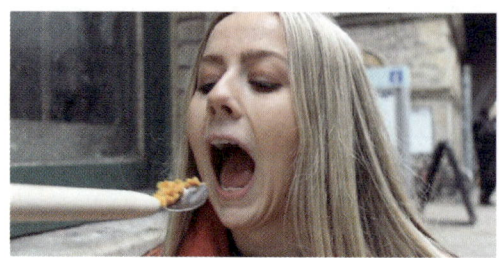

In the allegory of the long spoons, people in heaven and hell are presented with a bountiful banquet but only long spoons with which to eat it. Diners in hell twist and moan in starvation, blinded by their greed, as they are unable to feed themselves with the oversized tools. In contrast, diners in heaven fill the hall with laughter and chatter, consuming the feast by feeding one another with the long spoons.

Allegory of the long spoons was an interventional performance, exposing the interlinked transactions of intimacy and trust through food. Despite increasing the physical distance between two diners and the exposure of an unlikely public setting, closeness was created through the introduction of an unusually long tool. The double-ended utensil was negotiated and navigated between the two diners, reliant on one diner feeding the other.

Format	Performance, film
Location	Station Square, Peckham Rye, London

Sara Lohse *Musings on the Market*

```
FADE IN:

EXT. 25 ELECTRIC AVENUE SW9 8JP - 7.00am
A gentle rain falls onto the pavement of a relatively empty
Electric Avenue. It rained heavily last night - most of the
traders and shop keepers are yet to arrive. Rain drops echo on the
roofs of the few delivery vans that have managed to make their way
to the street.

A lone market trader has begun setting up in the middle of the
street. Metal scrapes on concrete as the trader quickly assembles
his apparatus. He takes a tarpaulin sheet out of a large blue Ikea
bag, and makes his make-shift rain shelter. The sound of rain
drops are amplified as they bounce off of the plastic and onto the
stone pavement.

30 second pass.

A mustard yellow delivery van pulls in to the street. It comes to
a slow stop across from number 25.

The noise of the van awakes K.M Meat and A.K Halal. Two friends/
neighbouring shops situated towards the east end of Electric
Avenue.
```

                                        K.M Meat Shop
'Amir?! Is that you? Have you come to open me up for the day?'

Silence.

                                          A.K Halal
'You know it's raining today, K.M.'

                                        K.M Meat Shop
'Thought my canopy was feeling a bit heavy this morning!
                                            ...
Amir will be running on rainy day time then…'

                                          A.K Halal
'Doesn't like the wet mornings does he, your Amir.'

                                        K.M Meat Shop
'Mm… could be the traffic.'

Contrary to many UK high streets, Brixton's Electric Avenue is buzzing; unit vacancy is low, with shops never devoid of customers. Interestingly, the street is almost exclusively comprised of independent Minority Ethnic Businesses (MEBs). The presence of MEBs on the street is important, reflecting the cultural make-up of the community and significantly contributing to the economic vitality of Brixton's town centre. *Musings on the Market* uses dramaturgy to narrativise the symbiotic relationship between these interconnected businesses, highlighting the infrastructural networks of mutual aid and solidarity that enable them to thrive in a rapidly regenerating neighbourhood.

Format   Script
Location Electric Avenue, Brixton, London

Lydia Hyde *Spiritual Kaleidoscope*

Format	Installation
Location	Central Saint Martins, Kings Cross Building, London

Comprised of a series of tall and acoustic oculi and visible and functional symbols, the *Spiritual Kaleidoscope* is imagined as a new infrastructure for spiritual space, which could be installed in public spaces across the city. The beacons stage a unique experience of the vertical space stretching between earth and sky. If churches are the cultural expression of religion, then the *Spiritual Kaleidoscope* is an experiment to try and create a cultural expression of spirituality as a physical space.

Annie Dermawan *City, Building, Body*

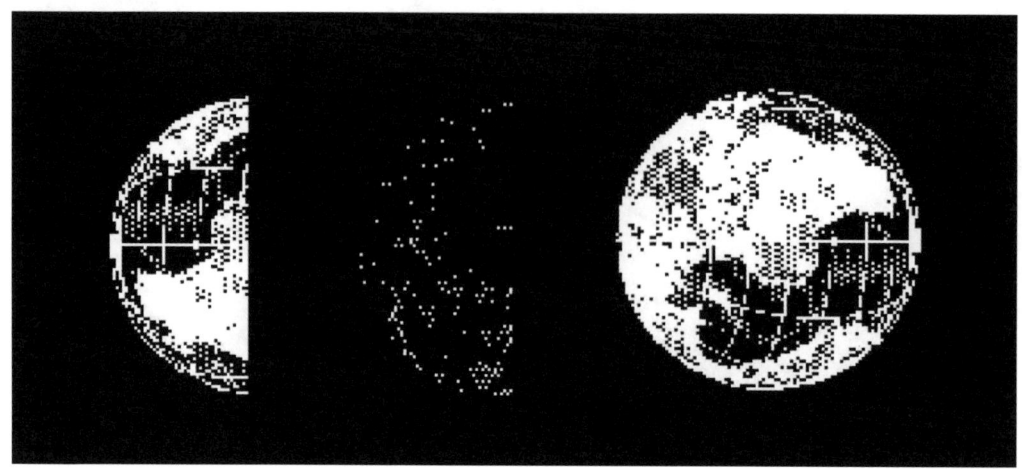

There's a moment
where you're stood with
hundreds of other people,

the music is so loud that you kind
of just lose yourself in it,

and you look around you, through
the strobe lights,
the smoke,

and you can see everyone is
just dancing

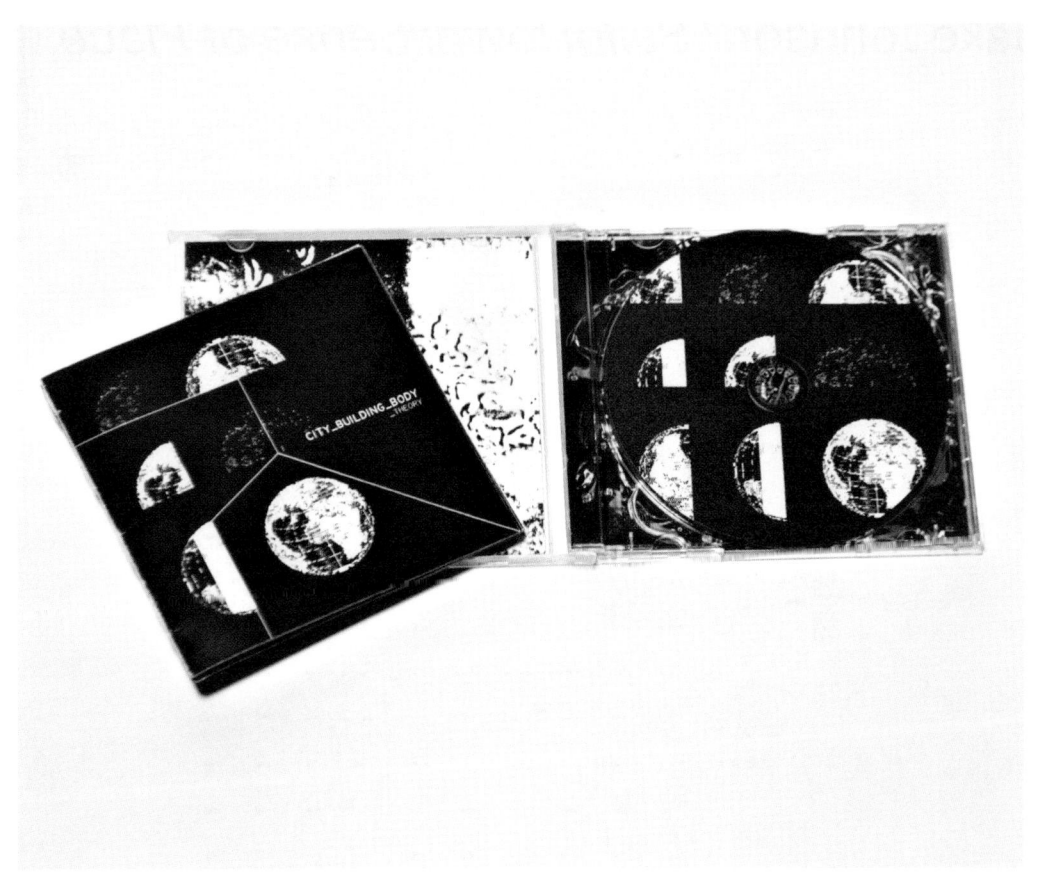

City, Building, Body plays out a composition of meandering memories told by active members of the clubbing community in the cities of Copenhagen, London, and Berlin. The piece addresses the role memory has to play in both creating and recreating stories experienced during a night out in a city and how club culture is influenced by the specific urban environments it evolves within. Snippets of stories are retold over the live atmosphere of a nightclub, in a sonic journey that brings these narratives to the present, voicing reflections on moments of shared reverie, hedonism, and euphoria.

Format	Audio recording
Location	Various nightclubs: Copenhagen, London, Berlin

Jake Johnson *Sailortown: Sense of Place*

Captivated by the industrial heritage of Sailortown, Belfast, this score seeks to record the material qualities of the area that contribute to its unique sense of place. In the wake of regeneration, it is imperative we retain spatial objects that significantly capture the spirit and history of these industrial landscapes. Dividing Sailortown into a quadrant can ensure a more meticulous and careful inspection of the urban fabric to reveal and record objects and materials whose patina and character capture the spirit of the place.

Using this score, spatial practitioners can ensure that these artifacts are retained in any future development and their historical significance is highlighted. White space within the score signifies the areas of recent or potential development, with the tension between the score and the void representing the friction between the local community and future development in the area.

Format   Score
Location Sailortown, Belfast

Performing Architectural Citizenship

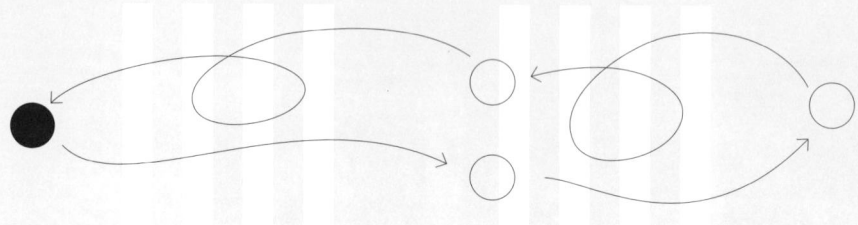

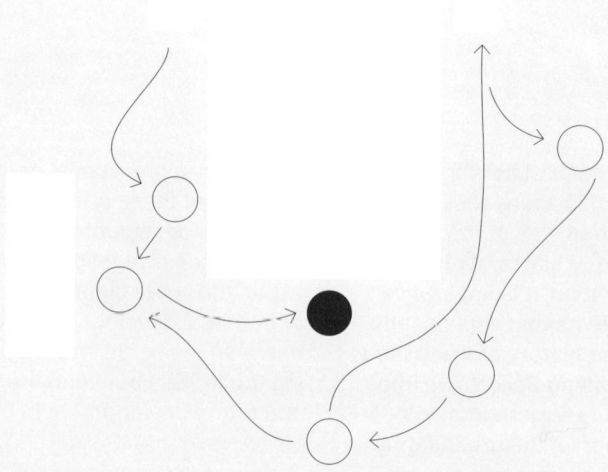

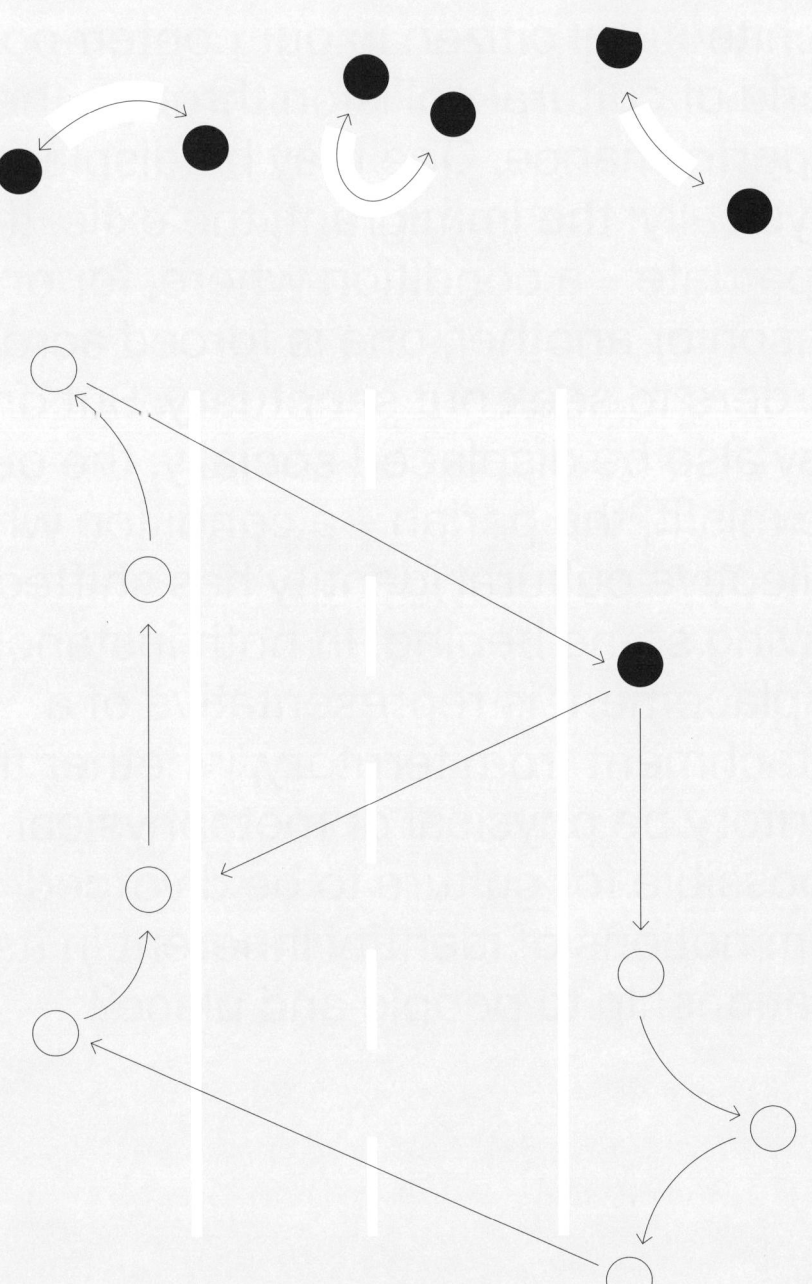

Performing Architectural Citizenship explores what it means to be an architectural citizen in our contemporary world of cultural collision through the lens of performance. One may be displaced physically: the immigrant, the exile, the expatriate – a condition where, for one reason or another, one is forced across borders to seek out sanctuary. But one may also be displaced socially: the outcast, the misfit, the pariah – a condition where collective cultural identity has shifted, leaving some behind. In both instances, displacement is representative of a detachment from territory, whether that territory be physical or metaphysical. Is it possible for culture to be divorced from notions of identity inherent in its relationship to people and place?

Mollie Griffiths
Rebecca Faulkner
Callum Brown
Dhara Bhatt
Awais Ali
Olivia Sutherill
Yibeijia Li

2019/2020

Mollie Griffiths *If these streets could talk*

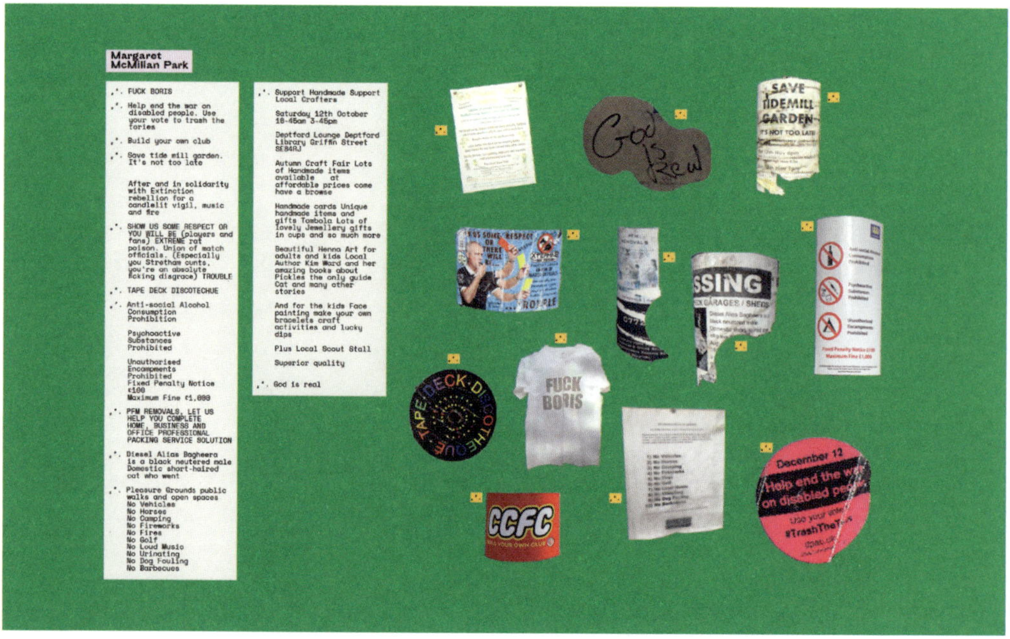

Deptford is an area currently undergoing intense urban regeneration. *If these streets could talk* critiques existing forms of community consultation, often a process where once a development has been decided upon by an external profit-making entity, the 'community' is asked its opinion with the promise of shaping very minor decisions within the place.

Instead of asking predetermined questions, *If these streets could talk* seeks to give Deptford itself a voice, creating a catalogue of the posters, stickers, graffiti, and adverts that appear in the public realm across Margaret McMillan Park, Douglas Way, and Deptford High Street. The catalogue became a script personifying each street, which played as a monologue over a filmed walk across the territory. The film forms a folk archive, a chorus of voices that subconsciously feeds into our perception of the neighbourhood and uncovers its hopes, desires, beliefs, judgments, and secrets.

Format   Film, catalogue, spoken word
Location Deptford, London

Douglas Way:

- REVOLVE
- BALAMII
- Albany Gardening Club

  Would you like to learn how to grow your own food?
  Then come and join us every Thursday and the last Saturday of every month for our gardening Club No experience Necessary. All equipment provided. All ages welcome. Children under 16 must be accompanied by an adult.

- BE ABLE - NO LABEL
- ASHWOOD ON TOUR
- You can have NHS or you can but you can't have both

  Vote tactically

- Support your local refugees
- Non Violent
- Balamii
- Vote tactically
- Anti-social Alcohol Consumption Prohibited

  Substances Prohibited

  Unauthorised Encampments Prohibited

  Fixed Penalty Notice £100
  Maximum Fine £1000

- Defended Autonomous Spaces
  Protect Your Future
- FTR
- I <3 EU
- Stop the holocaust in the Med - all borders are RACIST borders!
- Smash (immigrants welcome) Racism

- DONE
- JOBS

  We are recruiting

- You Asked me how I doing
- Keep Clear

  129 129

- Buy & Bye
- In times like this, the monsters come
- Deptford X FRINGE
  FRINGE FRINGE FRINGE
  FRINGE FRINGE FRINGE
  FRINGE FRINGE FRINGE
- Percy volume six mingle Bryan gee history of v waves arms sound system man like morgan bluetoof b2b izco djmc b2b moss. gsafe. richie
- Vote Labour then remain

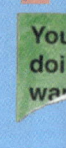

Rebecca Faulkner *A Dance in 8s Interludes*

In the public realm, dance and choreographic thinking can expose how social and spatial meanings and values are produced. When deployed in the city, choreographic thinking can offer tools to reframe the urban condition.

A Dance in 8s Interludes explored the convergence of time, space, and place within a site-specific location; the borderland of Hackney and Islington. The green man allocated only eight seconds to cross, suggesting ubiquitous and hasty movement – rolling or crawling were out of the question. At the intersection, pedestrian movement is conventional – sticking to the designated crossing points defined by 180 x 90mm dashes. In this collaborative performance, the dancers' embodied way of moving was harnessed as a tool to understand an instance of the public realm whilst critiquing the hierarchy of vehicular and pedestrian mobility in the city. For a series of eight second interludes, dancers, street objects, and unexpected audience members were momentarily united, creating a shared and collective awareness.

Format	Choreography, film
Location	Islington and Hackney boundary
With	Leilah Williams, Fabian Jackson

Callum Brown *Conduct to Conduct*

In *Conduct to Conduct* an activity is directed in which a person behaves to transmit energy around a particular place. This performance is assembled around acts of conduction. In analysing the material systems that exist in construction environments, much of the work has orientated around passages of energy and how the body can manifest or contribute to these systems. Mercury acts as a conductor in lights. Chewing foil allowed the body to replicate this conduction between two foreign metals. 'Conduct' entails a number of etymological derivatives that can be strung together to navigate themes of transportation, transmission, energy consumption, and human labour.

Format	Film
Location	Dungeness, Kent
With	Jemima Thomas and Matt Gabe

Dhara Bhatt *Housework is work*

(PHASE SPACE 2 - Service - Breakfast - Possibility B)

Vikas's plate is attached to TV stand, and the sieve is attached to Vikas's plate. He grabs a remote and switches on the TV. He slides down to the floor, pulls out the mat and takes his seat in front of it on the floor. He switches to the news.

Anjali   takes out Vikas's plate from under the TV stand and places it to the front of the mat, putting his food on it. Vikas adjusts himself around the plate and finds a comfortable position, then begins eating.

Anjali   grabs the food and tea from the kitchen and places them on the mat. She gets a saucepan of tea from the kitchen and approaches the mat with Vikas's mug.

Anjali   Would you mind picking up your toast for a second, just need to pour your tea.

Vikas   [confused, lifting up his food and waiting] Yes, okay.

Anjali pours the tea through the sieve into Vikas's mug and returns his plate along with his tea. She puts the saucepan on the floor and goes to get her mug and other snacks. Vikas begins eating again.

Anjali   approaching Vikas: I'm going to need to use the sieve again.

Vikas   sighs and sits back waiting. Anjali pours her tea and takes the saucepan back to the kitchen. Anjali comes back and looking for a space, sits in the centre of the edge of the mat facing the TV.

Housework is work situates itself in the realm of gender and domestic hierarchy in the context of Indian immigrant families in the UK. The project uses scriptwriting and role play as a tool to engage with the everyday rituals and 'directions' that enable hierarchies to play out within this ethnic group, using the nuclear family home as the stage upon which to examine the embedded gender dynamics of domestic labour.

Through a collective process of editing with collaborators from a similar cultural heritage, a pervasive theme emerged that reaches across cultures: whilst our cities run on these vital hidden infrastructures of care, the value of housework is still yet to be formally recognised or waged. The project seeks to challenge the patriarchal hierarchy, amending the script to create an imagined reality which empowers women entrenched within an ideal of 'female duty'.

Format	Script
Location	A family home, Leicester

She hovers around the kitchen while the tea brews, getting other bits prepared After a few minutes, she switches off the gas for the tea.

He uses the plate left out to do his prayer ritual; he takes the deity statue from the temple and bathes it in the plate laid out by Anjali.

Awais Ali *Multi-Generational Play*

Format   Choreographed play
Location   Cody Dock, East London

Multi-Generational Play uses choreography as a medium to facilitate a shared and common experience between the older and younger generations. Based on research conducted as part of workshops at the Story Garden in Somers Town, this performance used a vacant site at the Cody Dock in East London as a rehearsal space within which to test new forms of intergenerational play through the use of low-cost props and spatial interventions. The props require cooperation between participants, instigating new forms of shared movement, exchange, and engendering mutual trust.

Olivia Sutherill *Tipping Points*

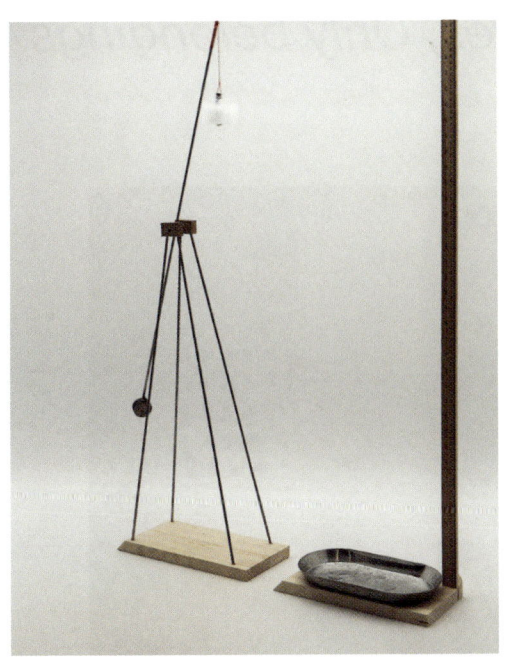 

Format	Installation
Location	Central Saint Martins, Kings Cross Building, London

Tipping Points is an installation that explores cyclic seasonal displacement, inspired by the methods of construction used in indigenous portable housing techniques. The structures of First Nations people are often bound together with ties or slotted together – techniques that were replicated in the installation. *Tipping Points* fulfills a dual role. Firstly, the structure performs by itself and operates as the 'actor', aiming to convey the idea that communities and individuals can reach a tipping point, a very specific moment in time from which spirals a chain of often rapid events. Secondly, the structure echoes the ecological conditions that processes of cyclic seasonal displacement are subject to; the properties of packed wool become a tool for the slow release of frozen water.

Yibeijia Li *No properties, Only belongings*

No properties, only belongings is a project that explores the notions of home and travel through documenting the ephemeral – collecting memories, experiences, and stories. The performance was conducted with seven participants, each of whom shared the common experience of living far from home. It started with the act of collecting a suitcase of meaningful personal objects, which were then catalogued. Objects were chosen for their emotional resonance over their functionality, and through a process of story exchange, the memories connected to them were teased out and shared.

Format	Installation
Location	Safehouse 1, Peckham, London

Contributors

Jayden Ali is the Founding Director of interdisciplinary practice JA Projects and works at the intersection of architecture, urban strategy, art, and performance – with a particular interest in working with briefs that directly engage with contemporary society and have a public offering. Previous projects range from architectural masterplans, to the production of documentaries and the establishment of community institutions. He is currently a Senior Lecturer at Central Saint Martins, a trustee of Open City (Open House), and an advisor to Theatrum Mundi.

John Bingham-Hall is Director of Theatrum Mundi and an independent researcher interested in performances, infrastructures, and technologies of shared life in the city. Since 2015, he has initiated projects with Theatrum Mundi on cultural infrastructure, urban commons, political voice, and sonic urbanism. Alongside this, he has collaborated on research projects at LSE and Oxford University; taught at CSM and UCL; published writing across scholarly and arts platforms; and organised queer cultural events.

Andrea Cetrulo is Associate Programme Curator at Theatrum Mundi, where she specialises in research, design, and has an affinity for architecture, philosophy, the Atlantic Ocean, and wine. She studied Sociology at the University of Barcelona, and Urban Studies at University College London.

Cecily Chua is an Associate at Theatrum Mundi, where she specialises in research and editorial. She has a background in architecture and her works focuses on the cultural life of our towns and cities, seeking to understand people's lived experiences of their urban environments and the subcultures that evolve from them. Her work has been exhibited internationally at the Architecture and Urbanism Biennales of Seoul, Buenos Aires, and Glasgow.

Elahe Karimnia is an Associate at Theatrum Mundi and focuses on urban research and spatial practice. She is an urbanist/architect, engaged in practice, research, and teaching at the intersection of urban design and critical theory. She is interested in plural narratives and multiple temporalities of cities and their publicness. She has a PhD in Urban Studies from KTH Stockholm, an MSc in Urban Design, and an MA in Architecture. She has worked in Tehran, Stockholm, Toronto, and London.

Andreas Lang is Course Leader and a Course Tutor in M ARCH Architecture. He has taught architecture at numerous institutions since 2001 including the Architectural Association, Sheffield University, The Royal College of Art, and Umeå School of Architecture in Sweden. Lang is the co-founder of public works, a non-profit critical design practice that occupies the terrain between art, architecture, and research. Working with an extended network of interdisciplinary collaborators, public works aims to rework spatial, social, and economic opportunities towards citizen-driven development and improved civic life.

Andrea Luka Zimmerman is a Jarman Award-winning filmmaker and artist whose engaged practice calls for a profound reimagining of the relationship between people, place, and ecology. Focusing on marginalised individuals, communities and experience, their engaged practice employs imaginative hybridity and narrative reframing, alongside reverie and a creative waywardness. Informed by suppressed histories, and alert to sources of radical hope, the work prioritises an enduring and equitable coexistence. Andrea grew up on a large council estate and left school at sixteen.